The Day in Moss

The Day in Moss

Eric Miller

Fitzhenry & Whiteside

Fitzhenry and Whiteside Limited
195 Allstate Parkway, Markham, Ontario L3R 4T8

In the United States:
311 Washington Street, Brighton, Massachusetts 02135

www.fitzhenry.ca godwit@fitzhenry.ca

Fitzhenry & Whiteside acknowledges with thanks the Canada Council for the Arts, and the Ontario Arts Council for their support of our publishing program. We acknowledge the financial support of the Government of Canada through the Book Publishing Industry Development Program (BPIDP) for our publishing activities.

Library and Archives Canada Cataloguing in Publication
Miller, Eric, 1961-
The day in moss / Eric Miller.
Poems.
ISBN 978-1-55455-084-5
I. Title.
PS8576.I5372D39 2008   C811'.54   C2008-900069-2

U.S. Publisher Cataloging-in-Publication Data
(Library of Congress Standards)
Miller, Eric.
The day in moss / Eric Miller.
[96] p. : cm.
ISBN: 9781554550845
1. Canada — Poetry. 2. Canadian poetry — 20th century. I. Title.
811.54 dc22   PR9199.3M55 .2008

Cover and interior design by Karen Thomas, Intuitive Design International Ltd.
Cover photograph of moss cells courtesy of Laurent Penet © 2007
Printed and bound in Canada

1 3 5 7 9 10 8 6 4 2

For Ben and Wimmy

Contents

3.   Cameo

River willow

River willow

1. This crack willow, just who is she? Ophelia, I think.
No, she doesn't go mad—no, she doesn't go under. Wild
grape she fosters and fluently she grows, an antiquity and
an innovation in the ageless, though not timeless, manner
of trees, self-garlanded and garlanded by the grape.

2. Likewise, this willow's Narcissus lucky—drowning as an
eye might welter sharper for its own tears, finer he emerges
always, he flourishes.

3. In fact, Ophelia and Narcissus couple here, living above
and below the image, reaching down and reaching up in
one gesture. Not a fatal union, it endures—virginal,
invincibly. They sink unsinkably, unbreakably they break.

   On depth and surface they found their faith. On flux and
stasis, on each other's essence, which is the other's image.

   In specular fidelity, they double their fruit, the flowers and
the visionary birds.

   Nightly by their twined toes birds root hot somnolence,
roosting across the willow's lateral tendrils. As bright by day
as lamps, birds show the way to tarry in the hurry.

   Volatility, stateliness, wings and songs brood the metabolic
moment. They never go out of fashion, though behind it
and ahead of it.

4. Thus, as a duck on a nest at an hour without fear and
almost without weather, the willow rests on its own sweep
and the river's sweep, meditation in the midst of force.

5.   Here is tranquillity's suspense. Final conflict of peace. Victory that never recognizes victory—oh, the lie that victory is, war likewise. Nevertheless, the wind in the willow sings *Te Deum laudamus.*

6.   Into the liquid shadow of the river willow, Heraclitus slips, as into a processional shoe, a probationary foot. He thinks no one is looking.

       Steps once, twice, three times into the boughs of the tree, the shade of the tree, the well-painted semblance on water of the tree. Everything licks and flows as constantly as the font of infancy, which persists in every kiss and drink, which wells in the raised and golden robin's warble over May's grey and rosy dusk—a sigh that blushes, a blush that sighs, tremor, adherence, lustred flicking of cadent hair. We know wrong, we want to know it and simply by touching forgive it, encompass it and (with mercy and simple hands) we establish mutual measure. The judgement? Here is the judgement: Embrace. The body submits to such radical comprehension. Some shame is high audacity, embarrassment fades twilight before the singular contour and gravity of the incremental flesh. Once there was cruelty, wasn't there? Touch is a different justice. Like song, like water, like light, cruelty runs away, not cowardly but soluble. Sophistry would attempt to collect it in recrimination and rhetoric's sieve. What does it catch? Crime is already drawn from one element into another, as into an afterlife. As remorselessly as love, verdicts evaporate.

The robin's warble passes over the brim of sound, out of the prolific sleep of silence, motif for all subsequent musics.

Such lucidity steps backward at the same pace with which time, that fountain, streams forward.

For leaves are a kind of root, roots a kind of leaf.
And sensation is reflection.

Petal fall

What *are* they? Petals,
petals that are falling.
Not the petals trees once detained.
Do they prove that the gust
in fumbling us
solidly assesses us,
and that touch might heap up,
ardent placidly
in a corner of the porch,
under the window's blear exaltation?
Or are petals coinage minted
beyond denominating—
munificence effaced before featured,
balmy and gone
in the blink of an eye, themselves
the blink of an eye, something
of the eye in their gloss, something
for the eye in their lustre,
eye-catching without eye-paining,
a truce of the sun, wedding
the vendetta of the inorganic
to the wincing of the organic?—
as though in their marriage a siege were lifting, lifting,
and the Trojan horse wombed no warriors,
and aspirant peace plunged, bright-beaked, lost
to the eye—lost *in* the eye, the fire of the zenith.
The plum trees' bouquets tip, shake,
in the tremor forfeit
petal (is it?) after petal, great loss, glad loss

in a triumph nameable neither as victory nor defeat.

Fledging

The matted-leaf weave
of the frowzy-mouthed nest
this season's brood breaches
with the same reluctance with which,
implication by implication,
the forest under-storey deploys its frilly
crush of compressed and indolent biota.

All earth broadens into the bulk and shoulders
of a ground-nesting bird in the pulp of springtime,
she will not flush from her station
any more than a moraine's intense, immobile detritus—

sun gums each thread of every spider-web,
adhesive ardour, gelatinous, crystalline—

as sticky as feeding
lips, feeding lips

halfway from mother, halfway to loss ...

What can be made but love?—

ubiquitous, equivocal manufacture.

Keeping the appetites, like waves

It's iridescence that gets us through the day—

emerald neck of the pigeon as, erect, rosy-
toed (with a look sharp-wet as the glance of beaded
shaving-cuts), among grey puddles diluting
painterly guano's inexpungible palette,
the bird nuzzles, plucks its shiny, sordid
spouse's cheek, where the swinish ferryboat's
back-wash whitens the harbour green
to radiant solidarity with this sheen
struck from malnourishment and happenstance—

it's the wooing—the billing and the cooing—
of organic and inorganic as they shuffle their clotted
plumage to wallow after appetite's skipping light
that plucks the flighty sleeve, needy zephyr
advising: "In hunger go happier, in tattered
bliss quest. Glut your heart on the glimpse
of those who may live on bread alone
yet glisten like more than manna from heaven."

For time passes, time flashes through as many tints
as dye the tilting speculum on a fat duck's wing—
purple mirror that imparts its mood
with the image, the way a gull flaps
as weakly as a broken stem, but glides
through the exhaust of the weather like
courage proof against pettiness. And the mallard's
florid foot pedals beneath the lurching
stew of the bay like an organist's,
pumping magnifying pedals to make
the clouds sound their volume all the bigger
as their pigmentation grows subtler

beside the cove that shimmers like a dove's neck,
with subdued but protean portholes in the swell
at which the celebrity faces of the spectrum appear
answering emptiness with colours that change
just quickly enough to stir nostalgia for
their sundry forfeiture—and a complementary
expectation of their odd advent—keeping
the appetites, like the waves, in motion

seamlessly ragged.

Crossing Halifax harbour

1.

Liner, dredge, tug, frigate, freighter.
So persuasive is their profile this morning
the illusion is every ship
is the unsinkable rock of ages,
whereas waves incorrigibly
caper and fling off fine
scales, skins, feathers, confidential
divestments across the swell's
looped, rolled and chequered volatility.
Water is as exhibitionist as fire,
Greek fire, a briny torch
aflame with revelation, flirting
with nearly recurring images
close to kissing, compounding
burlesque and enigma; everywhere
aqueous lips shape, press
for a fuller word we feel,
that drowns, laughs, blazes.

Sequinned the harbour shimmers, plumed
half Leviathan and half phoenix,
cormorant peacock,
Galatea swims here dissolved,
salt divinity and perfect flapper
swaying as on heels eternally
tipsy in her lucid drink.

But the ferry bears its weight of commuters
immune, mostly, to the call
of tidal flightiness, lustre,
undulant fixture, thick fluidity,
no mortal will seize that dazzling waist.

2.

As bright as a girl's portrait in a porthole
sun focuses through puffs of smoke
that a factory stack, striped red and white,
pastes upon the sky. The harbour bridge
strung like a harp sustains
every note
peeved traffic
advances. Poor morning,
lavish, poor: effervescence tosses
garlands and grape-clusters
at the ferry bow, dainty
tumultuously,
as by bursting dolphins
heralded
in ticklish rupture-rapture
our passage spatters us
with a rider's blithe lymph.

Involve in foam your bubbling gaze.
Amid inflation of the sea a souvenir
could recrudesce, consolidate—halcyon clutch
hatching or plump loop of puffed-up
pearls piped out of the brine's protean
blow-holes to drape a throat, slithering
Galatea in flecks and gems of spume, spit
distending from the thronged sub-undulation...

Onto a medium of such ebullience,
ether skids down like a duck
and pelagic depth breaches
whalishly and the bow's cobalt

paint and rust and oblique gull guano
butt aside the durable flouncing
of a froth more permanent, impermanent than we.

3.

Flocks dot the harbour like bright rocks
in a rockery. Then, trickling feet
up-tucked, birds circumflex
the silver transparencies, silver
opacities of the mist's inclination
to lead day-radiance down gilded
ladders to bathe a star
in stateliness of inklings
fully as circumstantial
as the barnacle-chapped wharf-piers,
whine of tire-buffers, consecutive
clanking of chain-links, cables, winches
that like fate catch the ferry subduing
us to our destination
while offshore Galatea still imbibes
the fond liquor of her bliss
and in her heaven is not quenched.

-

A snail trail glistening after

1.

The snails ride into sight again,
war-horses of patience at a stretch
budding gluey care
into self-exploratory air

and the worms, long and little,
move glint-ringed through puddles
like hands on love, slowly
where what is earth and what is water
remains intractably debatable in a tepid light.

And where the leaves smell of broken rules,
where the enamoured conceal their ooze and games,
foliate warblers invent old sounds
along ruptures and lean tips
and at the same time
in the music-naming mind
where remembrance and oblivion
look each other soft—hard—
and soft and hard
once more in the cloudy mirror of the ear
and shadow fits again to what has cast it.

2.

Growing pains occasion painful beauty.
Could there be a king Tantalus
whose reaching is repletion

as here where the crack willow hazards a bough
rippling to consummate foreplay
though its prime mover, the wind, absconds,
eloping with abysmal azure?

And, dead though it appears,
spotted with its own bark's defection,
the willow splinters, vivacious wistfully
like eyes tears have rarely ever left.
Leaves split to manumit
mucus tracts of nakedness
that clothe the world's more widespread,
desolated nudity and dress the long-stripped eye:
we witness the very operation
by which Ariel was tweezered
from old torment's heartwood.
Humid music swells from the air
amid tunnels sophisticatedly
fashioned from the night's
new-discovered foliage.

3.

The wind's lovemaking touch all over us
we cannot reciprocate, yet such largesse
rolled over our nerves
ennobles our aspiration
with the thought and feel
of such varicoloured flashing.

We want to have and hold the weather's inner snail-shell
          lustre
against which our senses clutch as hopelessly as a Sisyphus
who loves his stone as his sweetheart.

Bright, sap-and-sweat-dappled,
the darling ball rolls away.
But even its weight again relapsing
imparts glistering
shudders of delight.

Isn't erosion bliss to the falling riverbank?

Soul surpassing north

We couldn't help it—who can?
We went to the bottom of winter,
at whose glacial gates tears stall
and every breath must drive ghosts before it
opaque in the torments of their expulsion,
the stars in the sky meanwhile
wincing, but offering no succour.
We went to the bottom of winter.
What did we recover?

On the lowermost floe of the gulf,
we squatted and tried to remember lamentation.
Memory was frostbitten by oblivion.
Only its general shape was recognizable.
For love and mercy go through states like water
and at those glacial gates tears stall,
with reminiscence whitely blinded
like the frozen eyes of a fallen siskin.

But our black dog ran, claws
tintinnabulant, across the steely drifts
plated with the armour that the arctic rattles in.
The dog ran. She cast the weather's, the hour's
rigorous, indigo shadow.
The Romans called a soul *umbra*, a shade—
the dog threw just that, her heavenly-infernal *umbra*.

For there are depths like mountain-tops
in which every shade may shimmer
its prototypical posthumous flower
even in the midst of this, our flickering life.
And that is what the Ancients meant by naming
land past the reach of ordinary winter
hyperborean, blessed ... the Land of the Blessed,
of the most beautiful shadow,
pulcerrimae umbrae patria.

The dog wore a smile on her black lips.
Was her shadow a flag struck, or a flag raised?
We were alpinists at the season's core.
The dog planted a raggedy shadow
where the abyss equals the peak.
Beside the avid, night-dark, ghost-panting dog,
there chimed and burned a tract of *Aurora borealis.*

Zorgvlied, Amsterdam

1. Sorrows are fleeting. Or so we hope
    to the extent that we undergo
    rather than inflict them.
    Whence the name of the graveyard, *Fleeting
    Sorrows*, Zorgvlied.

2. And past the riparian gates of the place
    the Amstel parades the cozy houseboats
    of the coital rich, like sarcophagi
    mildly rocking, mildly on the shoulders
    of pallbearers all to testify that twice
    you cannot fuck on the same river

    though the poplars in reflection may promise the abiding.

3. Coots, whose young are black,
    tread pollution with red, lobed feet.

    Pollution asserts its own
    unfathomable purity.
    Almost like the clean flows the dirty, intimating:
    do not be so arrogant as to think
    you can truly harm the world.

4. But more beautiful than we
    remain our monuments. We can hardly
    live up to the gravity of everything
    that makes the world, including those things
    with which we have tampered,
    we thought decisively.

Poverty doesn't exist, the perceptible is the immortal:
such are the successes and deceits of every graveyard,
austerity being so sumptuous and loss
a crepitant lane under vigorously sighing trees.

5.   We don't have senses. It's that our senses
have us. This is what, for the most
part, keeps us going,
each of us a river of sensations
like a mirror that has depth.

6.   So even what appears to us as toxic
exalts us with its capacity
to be apprehended.

7.   So the three dimensions stand at the tomb
of Anonymous reminding us
KNOW THYSELF is a task none fulfills alone
and our beauty resides, like flowers
in a vase, like water in a bucket,
like a corpse in an open casket,
in a world that tastes us in true
ignorance of our own self-assessment

wherefrom comes that exquisite appreciation of us
which excludes us entirely.

8.   Poverty is wealth. Best, therefore,
the confessed exiguousness of epitaphs.

9.   And anyway, no learned attic that ever
went up in smoke
escapes its perpetuation
in the floating cypress-top
glossed by the queries of birds
whose voices vanish like sparks.

10.   Ants glitter like mica in search of steady rock
from which to glitter.
Up goes the tombstone like the fluke of a whale
and it is drawn, so slowly, down.

11.   But everything flows.
This the management of Zorgvlied knows.
These are plots, my friend, on which rent is due.
Seven years, and your corpse is turned out.

12.   Meanwhile, ten thousand turning leaf-
shadows mollify the rock of tombs almost like
Galatea wakening from mineral, a maiden
who might shiver from the North Sea stepping.

This material heaven uses.

Mud Creek

Whole. Whole and slim
as the thin ravine we enter. May green
gasps, leaks; we pluck snails
from sticking places, like laces
picked, wormed from the knot's
symmetrical inhibition.
Only lay them aside, let them
gum fresh station.
Through the grid of a manhole
gravel rings. It sings
Eurydice ... Eurydice and lightly
we sound (steep plenty)
the plummet of sundering futurity.
Queen Anne's gracious lace fringes
the culvert opening, where fast rats
pelter, wading stinking happiness, sluiced
tails as long as those of the grackles
that flash and blacken the air. At a finger's
tangency, pill-bugs pucker, take
cover, obstinate
balls of inordinate
nicety to exemplify
just how we open though
clenched, misgiving
giving way where the earth is wet.

Spring weeds itch in packed dirt,
pin-feathers rupture bitten skins in nests
woven as tightly as the ravine's
rank links. What have we done?
Naive thievery weighs the answer
thrust into a pocket from which
so much, subsequently,
may be drawn, as waters from a spring
as filthy and pure as the mouth, the heart.
O rat, O grackle, O lace.

Weave

Considered abstractly, the conjunction of hair and flesh
might have come off as off-putting, improbable,
but hard and languidly pressed the lax, follicular
floss—and the half-porous skin—convinces,
and you get spun into the spool of incarnation as such
as though hair were the thread from which warm, smooth, sweat-
and tear-coursing flesh really were woven.
Hair is the primal filament, skin the fabric
and the weaver wears the name of Care, for in the knit of flesh and hair
we feel always in the aura and nearness of care,
warmth from woken breasts, if not the young milk. Everything
that has been cared for, that is, whatever
lives, carries with it always the many who have thus far
nourished the one, the one whom we now
moisten, mumble, feed, eat, curl, part,
inhale, unravel, repair, repair and care for.

Diving

Tilted you stood so long you accrued
the look of a landmark, a conviction held
at once to make and to break the horizon.
Pondering your leap as though intent
had to mean more than any event,
like a cairn you balanced your life
or a crouched trunk temporizing, with an air of eternity,
over whether to topple or not,
surrender antiquity to dissolution.
The thought of cold water delayed
your plunge, postponed your change
as strongly as hands that might restrain you,
a presentiment of shock as hard as stone
yet as penetrable as the light-hearted clouds, all
convertible, with risk, with patience, to pleasure
after the shock of aqueous apotheosis passes.

Sky and ideas twisted on the lake.
Sundry eggs split in the shoreline's rocky nest.
Nuptial funerals of bugs like wet wings unfolded.
Day darted, day retrenched long, tingling, steep frontiers.
Shadow spilled and ran in clefts and troughs
of death and life, and as though a sacrifice
finally you fell forward into your own lineaments,
sheathed in yourself and the will to blissful pain
as though a coffin, chosen, could shatter into heaven.

With the thrashing of feet, commotion
like a flushed, massed merganser brood,
you foamed away, weather's aftermath or a current's,
and below you Atlantean outcrops bumped up as hills,
fish hovered, nudging herds,
bubbles phrased petitions, round bright hope.
A few kicks abolished land and mortal care.

Your respiration in the snorkel
(a singular pipe from the tales of Ovid),
amplified, rasped as ragged-palpably
as the water-weed that exalted jointed
lengths, like kites, to brush the swimmer
as devoutly close as the smoke of offerings, or a prayer.
Each foot flexed you forward with blended
velocity and slowness, you were
slowly fast.

Later, purple welts the mask
had impressed on your face confessed
your godhead, as on shore you streamed
bulky-wet as cataracts and cliffs. Yet
your children saw your divinity wrongly
when you dried, like something hatched again,
among capitulating waves, thin spiraea, the junipers
where vagrancies of butterflies blew
as petals, and mashed, spent mayflies
washed in the radiant pollen of the pines,
and your footsteps evaporated behind you

like apparitions after reason has dispelled them.

Among graves

What call can reach a girl
after (as deaf as the dead now)
she has found, found her felicity?
Harder than a sunbeam she smacks
the cemetery's sea-bright reach
of green. To be entombed means
nothing. Of memorials
what memory? Not urn, obelisk,
mausoleum, not the long plot
mounded over groundswell, margined
by chalky concrete, lichen-scabbed, tawny.
She cannot read and therefore
she stops to order, "Read. Read. Read it.
Read the name." Baulked she ponders
moss that cushions the mason's news.

Her coursing she resumes, antipodean
to lapidary, her heart and footsole thud
young fever, her sweat tartly sluices, she scuds
beside stone that grown-ups' reckoning
flakes away from. It's hair she savours of,
grass, furlings, dashes, tatters. But now like a weed
tap-rooted, the child must be pulled
out of this garden as mineral as Medusa's
by one stubborn arm, a limb reluctance
tangibly thickens, though without pain,
with reversions and looks hanging back
as though sentiment hovering
twisted her on green-tainted heels
to halt, dote on some past or future dead there,
interred. Her eyes yearn where lately
her cleats compressed tolerant moss and lawn
among memory's still, arresting,
incomprehensible conventions, harder than rock.

The conception of Achilles

The conception of Achilles

When the nymph of the straits lay spent on the sand,
her thighs apart, what staggered sense
was the slickness of her inner self
and the drier crumbs of the outer world
that so roughly clung to her.

How could she host such moisture and such aridity?
My hands liked both. But the blood did not have its source
in sand's abrasion, though it imparted colour
to the grains that stuck, and would not desert her.
I brushed them off, each dyed by her—fine Tyrian dye.
She seemed soft beyond expression, softer even
than wind-still water, than water gently entered,
but lightly coated, sifted over in places
with a reminder of the resistance of the world
(that irregular small aspersion of beach sand)
and the pigment inward to her gaze fused into the sky
and her rocking became an aspect of the waves
and what held me back made me go forward,
a membrane like time that we break, break again,
without meaning to, in a sense without effort,
though sometimes, baffled, favoured, we feel an effort,
also the fact that no effort's necessary,
time goes on with us, goes on without us
amid the sea lettuce, the bladder wrack,
tongued bulbs of kelp, where the window-pane cool
sea-glisten slides forward and pulls back,
lovingly viewing and mauling the place between places
so rich in shelled and mucous life
delighted to be tousled and to be fed

even by a mortal, though she is immortal,
intact at the next tide by which we may be swept away.

The playground

In the morning, the reality of seeds
jabs, makes points and is most
prominent. Acorns and chestnuts
like munitions lie scattered
over the late-lush grass, over dampened sand.
How improbable they should ever
dig down or be buried
beneath densely grass-woven and foot-packed
rebounding, unbountiful surfaces.

This wooden act of reproduction,
impervious children of trees—they look as sterile
as rusted rocks of bloodless Mars,
as parched Carthage sown with what
seems to be
conclusive salt.

Yet cold high care condescends
to consummate the scene,
thinly fulfills the empty dew,
pregnant each void bead
with nothing, excepting itself.

Then acorns loom, and chestnuts swell—
the clear peers of trees.
Generation's no cycle, nothing
to do with growth, but a sequence
without priorities or consequences,

as though the ladder that the kids climb to the slide
revealed each rung as distinct, incommensurate,
neither a way-station nor anarchy.
No one may mount the scale of being.

The dynasty is instant. Acorns, oaks:
the harvest may be hard, but it does not sting.

My children's feet fall again
to the unyielding surface, to the earth that yields.
Good and evil are equal.
They have every
and they have no relation.

The bridge

Without thought, we started to cross the bridge
trusting in the piers that, unseen, supported it.
Eclipse, annulling origin and terminus,
singled out our stretched hour. Thrusting beside
the silver sandstone of the balustrade
white oak crowns widened like quenched
torches, antecedent even to the city—
each one the hunched curator
of chill nests tight clinched
that might survive the toppling of the trunk,
like wreaths more durable than the grave
they cannot hope to prop.
We paused over the middle,
obliteration vivacious at either end,
to either side a gulf. A gulf above us, too,
where star clusters mimed abrasions of love
damp, and stinging, slipping
into a rash of precocious remembrance.
Smoky rustle of autumn leaves spiced the stooping air
with the humble leakage of human love by night.
Where was the end of the bridge?
Our feet must evoke it, by the clasp of our hands
on top of gulfs, below them, beside them

for nothing human, though it spans a valley,
stands on more than a memory and an idea.

Middle age

In us (whatever our age) is middle age, slow, vulnerable
to the obtuse boot, and always wet like a licked lip but at its peril
wet, as an untended birth under moist stars retracting their damp
blessing like the slug's horns, fungoid, imbellicose.

The slug, middle age, looks like something spat from the mouth
with a cough of disgust, or in the uncouth joy of phlegm expelled.
The phlegm is ours. It is the morning's and inalienable,
jellied and chill, like a genital impassioned by abstinence,
pleased by its long-impacted orgasm, savouring
the ingrown shell of erotic ideals, self-absorption sufficient oil.
Yet strangely solid it still travels, pilgrim of disappointment
ravished by glue and narcolepsy. And look at the slurped
track of torpor it leaves to crackle like masterly varnish
in a later sunlight, drawled behind as a slack mouth's spittle
soaking the worn case of a motel pillow.

There it is, over there—the bad cold cut at love's sylvan symposium.
Ah, even the omnivorous, risqué jays ignore it.

Epitaph: the Passenger Pigeon

Don't condemn them. Chances are you're
no better. But ask: What were
they hunting, after all? They answered
The Passenger Pigeon and took the money, every
red cent, and packed the hundred thousand
bushels onto the waiting train, the percussion
of whose transit shook lopped trees
in tempo the whole way over the horizon,
which smoked. They aimed, they fired,
they hardly tired but there was something beyond
the recurrent bird who entered the trajectory and dropped
below the narrow barrel stricken, fluttering like
the cloth that mimes *I surrender*. The pigeons, it seems,
and continent capitulated.

                But they had trained
their sights, I'm sure, on something else besides,
and by the hour the pigeon had died five
billion times (the last in a zoo, in Cincinnati),
the religion that first convoked the hunters
was gone like Christ and the mild bald clouds
burst through the savage aviary roof and rolled
the size of hills over the tomb of the land
laying and peeling brilliant shrouds as big
as Gotham. Yet, though the rafters of old forest
were fallen, was the veil rent?—No, it won't be
until the knowledge dawns on what they'd trained
their sights, they who must have hunted something
else, *guns so hot we were afraid to load them,*

and behind the veil the end, if it is an end,
clarifies like day and like a seed and
visible from far below, as a cipher
shining through a crosshatch nest, precariously
germinating, high in the solid spectre of an oak.

Northern phoenix

Chill over it, chill below it,
aloof, diminutive the diving duck
trimly lifts again—a phoenix dim
imminence of ice rears, bears up
beyond land and leaf-furring frost
in the slushy pulse of the sea's wallowing—
hypothermia's wan, bold fog and wash
effacing vital signs, penetrating
(you would think) that well-greased plumage.
We hold our hot hearts tight
but though our feet believe in rock,
it, too, will split like the brine's
ubiquitous gorge to swallow
our jutting bones, our tenuous heat.

Or we'll rise again. Like the merganser.
Not from aromatic, Arabian combustion
but from arctic sea-straits reeking
of something endlessly conceivable, rotten,
preserved from death, not from decay—
undiminished though decomposed.

Nothing dies. It dives or it flies.
The veined rock melts.
And the sun submerges like a diving duck
into the passing resemblance of permanence
that the sea wears always,
like a blank tombstone over which
drafts of an epitaph unkillably flow.

The pond

1.

The innocent have no need for absolution.
They love to get heavy, but not with guilt.
Where reflection multiplies in coolness,
meditation blunts, then revokes apprehension
and flashes liquidly back, drowning it in its origins.
Everything this morning advances a wet mirror.
The cold wet brims passionately
as though tears were tears and remained entirely rational.
Without the wetness, there would be no mirrors.
From these drenched mirrors, justice shines.

The moisture of innocence is not mammal damp.
Nor is it reptile. It is the flow and gleam of reflection
in the innocence of water, which condones no lie
pronouncing so elemental a sentence.
And so the moisture condenses on the father and the son:
the duck's speculum, the pond's toils, the willow leaves'
lenient daggers and the candid lily pads
reflect in darkness, as in a glass beam darkly.
In these opulent, these confluent mirrors
all falsehoods collect, pool, dissolve.

Once we saw face to face. Can we now
slowly? Let patience of reflection exonerate.
Just when the sun is sent behind the cloud wall
and leftover radiance glistens, humane,
on the drippingly precipitated mirrors
do the eyes open, heavy-wet, to the image of innocence
in which we have always been made.

2.

The boy and the father saunter among mirrors.
Cyclopean stones ring the pool, their images swim.
Obscurity loads the stones, yet more liquidly—
as though a gravestone were already a resurrection—
they flow with the ponderous confidence
of a snail out of the city of the dead
in pursuit of the life after pardon
that knows no haste, sliding past death.

These mirrors reverse verdicts.
In casting back and forth such heavy themes and things,
the space between gains weight, sumptuously
innocent. It is in this trajectory, this passage
in the company of mirrors that space grows thick
with its having been travelled through
toward new judgement—toward clemency.

And the father's and the son's eyes
catch these thrown and halted heavinesses.
They become cairns of contemplation.
Their step is slow and grave with mercy.
Hand in hand, bonded by twined fingers, pressed palms
and hovering hosts of reflection,
they pause by the exculpating waters and reflect
as though tears were tears, yet remained rational.

Free as a bird

No. It's not that birds are free,
nor that we ourselves are free.
But, rather, that in the differently
imprisoned relation between the birds and us
liberty lives.

A cage? The free bird is caged
in adaptation to the prison, conformity
without submission, or in such submission—
decorousness void of cravenness—
that the discovery of similitude
in the pressure of necessity
is the freedom that we have,
acquiescing to everything
in every detail
as though as conscious as God.

In the image of what has to be God,
we are made and remade
saying "I feel as free as a bird"
which is no lie, yet a flight of fancy.

Then our fate, is it to perceive the destinies of the birds?
To perceive an alien destiny
is already in some measure
to evade our lot. It wasn't our fate
but we made it ours, we fly
alongside it and this flight
is brave and among these sounds
we sound no retreat.

Against the assumption of irony

1.

You're no more ironic than the bird that sits on a post.
It announces its name over and over again.
It thinks that this is the law and that this suffices
            against the universe's
music, the music of the spheres that is neither
sincere nor ironic, but unbreakable.

Look where the breasts are swollen with milk
and the mucous lips are moist around the moist chafed nipple:
that's clandestine you, sucking at the teat whenever you need to,
a sincere addict crying you're dependent on nothing,
yet your brittle mind in its cup is filled
by milk neither sincere nor ironic
that flows always with tears wan as stars, a pale food deaf
to the name that is your strengthless boast.
Well, it feeds you regardless, and never learns your name.
This nutriment is neither charity nor indifference.

And past you the music goes and you don't know a thing,
though deadpan wit may insist that it's smart, smarter than matter.
That music is where you came from and where you are going.
And every fibre of your being no matter how far you have travelled
has never left that music behind and soon you will face it fully
dissolved into milk, bone's melody, bone's harmony,
cascading through galactic black room that your mockery has not
                    once touched.

2.

The same things he says about his enemy also fit his friend.
Is that satire? Of whom, then—in the end?

47

Redwing

1.

The redwing is the crowing cock crying
not betrayal, but dawn hatching
from the calcified crust of every minute
as thick as cattails with a voice of quagmire
bursting from midair, a Vesuvian
blossom whose happy lava
puts to music a grebe's generative raft
loaded with a blanch-sided clutch and spiced
with the glitter of semi-precious flies.

Thus saith chrysalis, hymen, bud, gazing
mouth and lapping eye, which rupture
compulsively and compulsively re-heal
in the euphonious filth of little thunder
bombing the aeons with beginnings,
brooding the bog with ignited wings.

2.

But all marshes dry,
all blackbirds die.
What to do in such cases?
Believe in the desert—or the oasis?

As the flight of a swallow

Near us, yet far beyond hypocrisy,
the swallow swivels, airborne,
just as we, though we feign,
make no pretence, for deceit's
our nature, as flight's
the swallow's fluent resource.

Does wrong belong to the swallow?
Boldly, the swallow obeys whatever
in physics comes close
to that strange, allowable swerving.
But though it errs, it never
dissimulates. *Persist in the mistake*
sings the swallow, the swallow our sister.

A raving beauty the error is
at every pass. The forked tail flares, the eye
feels the tolerant sky
for the opportune aperture. The wing may,
like remorseful reflex, contract:
wincing's what flight sometimes looks like.
But air's impeccable, air's
immaculate. The swallow's brief,
wide, whiskered, eloquent beak chatters
like water and sucks the rich, thin sky,
chatters like water, sucks the thin, rich sky.

Avidity matches the zephyr's grace, fleet
and footless, pace for pace.
Grass, cedar in fever, compost's spice,
the snails' long vestige, water
that quenches the spotted dust, flowers
mottled, wilting, exhaling

their last appeal: wings over the garden
caress this sprightly, moribund
perfume—their harpsichord.
The atrocious hawk gives pause, but day
endorses it all, the mistake
is as real as the correction.

So the swallow, our sister, sings
What happens is always persuasive.
Whatever happens is always persuasive.
O slight, titanic wing,
can we have lived through, again,
what we cannot possibly have endured?
Strait was the gate, and somehow good.
The air is clear, and our conscience.
What are the claims of conscience?
In all conscience there are disclaimers.

Nothing before death is inauthentic.
Everything after death is genuine.
O devious candour.
O corrupt, incorruptible
frankness, comparable in complication
to the ravenous, whimsical swallow's flight.

November rain and song

Vituperative November. Yet the robins are voice
over voice, voice into voice coalescing and diverging
in a light cut with rain, rain cut with light, a hard sun's light,
light as solid as a thrown stone
or like the fractured columns of the rain.

And void dim dire water as it plunges hits the birds' song, driving
those sounds like struck insects aside, yet letting them resume their course
as a drop slams a stiff leaf and the leaf bounces
brightened coldly and coldly resilient,
deflected though returning to its first inclination.
The flocks sing, and the listener's cold hands
through the sculptural suspensions of song
feel the swathed, tinted heat of one robin's breast
pressed between them—taut instrument from which
musical steam and streaming music issue, despite interfering weather.

And how was it, anyway, that blood could warm itself
in the first brave, separate secession and instance,
circulating darkly, brightly to warm the breath and warmly impart the music
from so many lonely, sociable stations
scattered by austere estrangements of animate fate?

The pillars of water match exactly
the lifeless temperature of the universe
and despite its catapult of rays
the sun has got no warmer
with the friction of its compulsive missiles.

But in chill branches and in sky that chokes on its own cold blood,
self-warmed life spills note after note

onto an earth
that largely denies life's heat and praise
clasping them always firmly, deafly
with the imminence of a negation.

Cameo

Cameo

Bonne amie, I flower with sweat again
rejoicing like one who, weeping,
can feel grief finally
oozing, spurting—coming, and leaving
solicited, sucked and wiped away
by the blonde thirst and *tendresse* of an ardent climate.
Just as stodginess shucks its costume hiking a hill
(heat staggering decorum),
so magnanimously I toss
tears of sweat to inaugurate
fresh clemency of life
like Tacitus beginning his *Agricola*
"Now at last returns our heart ..."
malignant emperor Domitian dead.

Now at last returns our heart, sonorous
in the throatiness of the mourning doves
whose tails taper like ribboned pig-tails
from Boucher, Watteau, from Fragonard,
whose wings whimper and simper
(each bird its own dextrously handled fan),
beauty-patches, obliquity in the pine allées,
topiary trimmed by wild nature's
savage-judicious hand—
beaux and *belles* and *billets doux,*
the Eighteenth Century languidly avid and dulcet
amid the blushy-barked conifer bowers,
and quite frankly I like it
(even if I have annotated sundry
polemics against Sensibility
dizzy and slipper-dandling on my giddy swing).

For the *fair sex* is everyone.
The *weaker* the *vessel* the *better*.
Rousseau was right.
Morals, they're *botanical*.

Robins' bosoms ease and force on us
their auditory blossoms, dogs gape
whiskered, gummy runnels and crocuses
sprawl purpureous
growths of after-
pleasure, hoses nod water
on the tonguing beds, I sigh like a dove's
coquettish wing-tips
curtseying among the forest's amorous wellings,

from all of me slide long tears of resumption.
Where was I? Where was I? The day perspires
kisses, shadows are stage go-betweens while
the venereal doves carry twigs to the yolk of my central coo.

Niagara

1.

A diarist relates that, one summer afternoon in 1793, cruelty
assuming its usual form, human, strolling
along the shore of the Niagara River, loosed
from a dock the canoe in which a Mohawk
slept. It appeared to be an instance of straightforward, mocking
murder and the one who undid the knot never
was detected. Loiterers on the bank, wishing in idle panic
to effect a rescue, could not—could not but watch as the man, waking
at the motion of the current accelerating,
sat up and absorbed his fate
as a stone the sun's touch,
dry in the midst of a surging stream. Delectable
day, cool, confiding the flow, the rapids still far off,
though hunched in the distance immortal
water crouched crumpling for precipitous aeration.
The man sat still—a figure on a medal struck, whom witnesses
called *stoic*. Strong as the epithet was, it availed nothing
against the current. Then what was he?
A man beautified by the imminent mortality of his profile
in a canoe contrived from the lambent bark of the birch
treated with pitch of conifers to forestall leakage.
His shapely, fragrant little boat was watertight.
Sweet as throaty doves the concerted water falling, sweet
the water that gloves and fits any dangling hand,
sweet to stir eye-bright water-birds from their racing seats on the water,
sweet to fellow the birds as you pass them blue and white
as though you, too, had, like paddles, paired and folded wings on your
    back,
sweetest of all to view the shore bountiful, successively, as love
rounding a body's bends.

Past helping's where you're pulled.

Yet he awoke unbruised at the base of the falls.

2.

A last efflorescence flushed my mother when, dying quite young,
her gaze cleared again, her complexion cleared, her voice returned
and she could still walk. She could walk with me. We walked,
her carriage upright, as upright as a birch tree's carriage, as a
    dancer's,
and she once was a dancer, and now she was frail, and almost I felt
I was taking a girl for a date. This girl made me proud and frightened
as though I held something too light and too heavy for my hands,
always on the point of dropping it from its fickle levity, gravity.
In her company I trembled like water, like light in the leaves of a
    birch tree,
water is the same, subtle, at any distance from the cataract,
she was the breeze that moves the water, that feels the humid
    foliage.

She sustained the interval between an edge-grown bending reed
and the image the shattering water tries faithfully to return to it.

3.

We strolled along Bloor Street in the falling sun.
The day flowed down like a great river lapping the grateful city.
How harmless the busyness of other people, their
busyness was our leisure, we did not descend beneath surfaces,
not even in imagination. Permanency fixed each person just
so—a bird in its ordained plumage, the ordained
festivity of its plumage. Fashion was truth, truth
fashion. No disguise, no dissimulation, nor yet a performance.
Everyone was immemorially and immediately *this*.
No moral distinctions, no histories, just the eddying transient mandate:
pleasure. I can't remember what my mother chose to eat.
Almost I felt that I was on a date—

but she looked out at the day, a canoe caught in a current.
Eye-bright, the stream shines. Like a drink it cools.
And, as with laughter, there is a vibration. Water
talks fluently its dear and estranging language
many-hued as a flock of buoyant confluent birds:

the Mohawk, whose name does not descend to us, lived.

4.

What a wonder routine talk is,
with a word it spans the gap
of so many years, such disparate conditions.
You may speak with a dying person
sometimes to the brink of death.
Who would believe in reciprocity?
Yet the proofs recur, they recur.

A withdrawing bird is the same bird
that once clung close and sang,
a feature of your heart.
The eye keeps the departure in view;
departure, too, is an object of the eye.
So remote the bird! And ever more remote
but vision detains even diminution
as though it absorbed into a clear orbit
as into the walls of a womb
what was born and dies
and now seems never born, or about to be born,
borne away again on the delectable current
which falls, crashes and lives, as air or water
evidently unbruised.

The slacking of necessity

Fat rapture of fledglings has shattered
the flanks of lichen-spotted nests. Foliage,
it rasps tastily, like fabric at a *fête galante*.
Sap-damp cloth makes you appraise by guess
the thick under-dimples of limbs,
filaments, moss pungently clustering.

Breezes elaborated in oblique trees
tap passers-by with shadows. Bold
·that touch—how quick—how knowing,
as though they passed on a *billet doux*.

Shafts of light sound leafy valves that close
with the indolence of vireos' throats, which slow
their song's blurred ray and cease, because
song's solicitor, need, slackens into trance,
the sleep that caps a growth spurt.

Youth's gluttonous shape sprawls finished
on a plinth—a tree crown on its trunk.
A tree crown on its trunk relaxes,
an afternoon cloud prone, though robust,
to dissipation, caducities,
self-toyings of languor.

Coloured wraps bundling, barely, their repletion,
fledglings bulge, fed like shade with waving day.
Berries gather, a weight-gain of the breeze,
globed with gratuitousness, gorged
to realization. Antiquarian insects
stage a masque of varied classic costume,

glittering, flashing out history's
fashions, lightly. Wings, scintillae,
radiate from the river's fluent, cruising flesh.

How high our sighs heap the leaves' carbon harvest
while fruiting bodies, fattened on the smell of shadows, coalesce
in union with one another and their futures.

The Fall

What was the transgression? the accused can only ask.
Who noticed it? Felt it? Nature groaned—
was it a groan of rapture or of universal vitiation?
Pastoral it was before, pastoral afterward.
Eden never vanished, the idyll never faded,
the genre would not alter, comedy prevailed.
If a sword spun before the shut gate,
the sinners remained moist, remained loose in the garden state
sustained by the presence and presence of memory.

Judgement is failure, is miscarriage of imagination.
As for God, what caught God's fancy?
Divine hands compounded ambiguity with felicity.
Sin is innumerable, passing into salvation and out of it,
ascending and descending, descending and ascending.
Could God be victim of such violence,
such weakness, as to pass sentence?
To pass sentence is to annul
error's multifariousness, its coziness,
its glory, its refined reek, its grandeur,
to fix its opalescent, cascading memorability
into wisdom's unpliant platitude.
Within its walls, invincible Eden has no bounds,
a *hortus conclusus* without conclusion.

Didn't God transgress in imagining transgression?
That mistakes even exist vindicates them
as much as any other thing created.
Who but God imagined the Fall?
What fell falls and falls to happiness

though the verdict falls otherwise
bloodily, it may be, and heavily,
mortally, grievously, gravely,
so that deity itself cannot distinguish
murder from self-murder
any more than the judge may find more culpable
one or the other of equal confessors to a fault
at the advent—here it comes again—
of a false though fatal reduction.

It may be fatal, but the false passes:
yes, yes. This, too, shall pass and, like Eden, remain.

Fruit flies and clouds

Fruit flies manifest space, space odour-ample
through which they navigate, rebuffed
sometimes, toward the origin of scent,
though not toward the origin of space.
Watching the flies, you do not reflect on their organs,
compressions, seizings, wizenings,
innocuous semblance of ferocity.
You concentrate on their senses, how they perceive
immensity and fullness and vacancy
as you cannot, because size changes the fate
of experience. They embody room's
extension and volume
whereas the incumbent clouds
in their altitude, diffuseness and stony
opacity (which contradicts their vaporousness)
indicate, contrarily, the sky's majesty. A fallen
flowerpot is as capacious to a fruit fly
as the cliff-carved roseate city of Petra
where caravans paused among breast-plated centurions.

How long, vicariously, you may explore these hollows
tucked baldly in the breeze. So rummage
among the agitation of the fruit flies.
Twirl through the fruity air.
Lounge in the weather's confidently
idle immensities, its widely knit
hammock of twined light, drafts and shade,
veined vibrations of diaphanous wings,
aromatic rot's blur of apertures, vulvas, nostrils.
The day sunk into flagstones warms you.
The wind chills you with cold gestures of the tiny
climate. Your senses stir, dispersed
with fruit flies. Like clouds, they embellish their epics.

And, as a smell moves forward and back
on the hinge of the mobile weather,
birdsong sends its pipings intermittently
over the tilted palings of the fence.
So a faint diagram might grow
not larger or more complex, but denser.

Ashes, too, are fire

(Girl, 3 years old)

Fever-serious she probes the bed,
a liminal creature, without a shell,
under evasive waves of slumber,
and she seeks where bodily tides
turbidly equivocate
the running zone of sleep,
body hot and, through the heat, chill,
and her fingers flapping for a hold,
extensions
under or above
the medium they are best fitted for,
as though aware of how little purchase
we ever have on one another, on the elements,
on health, sickness, night, day, ourselves.
I feel her rippling, the weakened pulse
of a spent surf, against my back.

Now I am a beach,
nerves dispersed like sand grains,
nerves ordinarily dormant
atomistically awakened.
Vigilance she quickens
even as she coils, she roots
obliviously for oblivion.
So she turned in her mother's belly.
Then, as abruptly as the arriving swell,
her three years of night blackly douse at last
her three years of day.

Along the shore, beside a fire,
people have drowned day's pain
around flames that resemble them.
The penumbra twitches on the crooked fuel
and, after bent bodies have darkened with sleep,
the fire fails. But the minds of the sleepers
do not fail. They have gone different, not cold.
In the sky and on the water
stars like sand are scattered,
but night unites them
palpable, untouchable,
unapproachable, whole and null.

The wake

Around rocks you steered the bow while
I sat at the outboard motor crowned
by its whipped-away, regenerating
garland of fumes. Gas's agreeable reek
the wind instantly pulled beyond full
inhalation, whereas from the shore
pine aroma welled indispellably
and lichen and moss respired, brimmed
the mounting smell of subsidence into
the perfection of intrinsic perfume
dense despite the bald prevalence of outcrops
and particular, somehow, in every breath
snatched from the serene yet accelerated air.

Always exhaust twisted off as swiftly
as the right solution to a recurrent problem.
Inside the engine roar as in reverie
 my own flailing hair flicked me,
like a tern that dives to defend its nest.
Our wake giantly sketched a triangle
in symmetry that often swerved.
Foam as thick as paint lifted—a mane of water
the propeller had turned, roused and tousled.
Choppily our geometry slacked off sideways,
gulping at lichenous rocks, dipping low tree lengths
where sparrows hopped over pure, distorted reflections,
in filamentous daylight moths clung and milled
like stellar plotters conspiring pallidly till night.

The motor swung bouldery peninsulas aside.
Cormorants sank like wrecks. Stones rose,
their frothy backs flapped by waves as by wings.
Cattail-recessed, reed-shielded shy things
beat on the water darkly web-striding, then slurred
to a breast-heavy halt and a lurch with stub tail up-fanned.

2.

Let the wake mouth every instep of the shore,
lap it, kiss it like a perfect foot, saturate,
put all of love in the mouth
and cup it all in transparent hands,
let touch itself be distilled and upswept
evaporated. And from the moisture so
transported as perfume let
condensation fatten, compounding
a bright cloud no
grander than our boat.

The warbler green, black, and yellow in the pines
is a home-made instrument in the illimitable afternoon
where the sun looses a wake of blue shadows, black sweat
that creeps along and somewhat coolly soothes

while loftily the cloud-hull undulates
into successive, diffluent pleasures
of azure dispersal, diminishing
increasingly

above where the planks of the dock and our boat quietly rub.

The work

1.

As Ovid tells it Pygmalion *conceived a love*
for his own work. *His own work ...*
Pygmalion conceived a love, but Galatea
he couldn't have conceived.
Haplessly belaboured
sculpture all remain
till caprice and fate concur
in a fluke
melt like between-
season weather when
temperature plays
reversible Medusa to water, sharpening and easing
her lock and breath
and water, like the body all abroad, flows.

Someone's hands impinge their pressure
and we are released, we sweat,
eyelessly our bodies sob, we drive
petrific time from our skins
and it departs like an army
of frozen occupation—to what
carver's credit is this excellent
deliquescence? It forgives us.

True, Pygmalion ached to cup the real
suspense of breasts whose swoop
and ductility
slides by stopless immeasurable
measures into the moist
nest of armpits and up to the turn

of shoulders that taper to forearms
and hands, fingers tenuous
yet articulate to lay down
feeling, craft or music where there had obtained
blankness, only
blankness.

2.

Concede to Pygmalion simply
capacity to appreciate, to stroke
and not to tire of stroking those volumes that could
mobilize and flutter hotter than blood
in the trusting, circumstantial
scuttle of nerves.
Thus hair at the groin may curl where stony
smoothness once baulked and the lapsing
solidities of breasts may tremble, mollified,
their marmoreal orbits of lucency
venereally stained.

Above the sweeping groove of the nape the twisted
uplift of hair may ravel and re-convolute, loose
from the lapidary, no longer decorative
in the pigmented springiness of questing light and hands
and odour lives there like the day in moss.

3.

It was only Galatea's divergence from the expectations
of Pygmalion that could disclose exactly the degree
of her pertinacious applicability to him.
As she came to the surface of her skin,
swimming to confront her own contours,
she sank away from the topography on which
his incongruous desire had insisted, which possessed
less ingenuity than the mass and filigree of its gathering
fulfillment whose increments are elusive—for
pleasure always flinches from its source—
which is everywhere, on all sides, and yet untouchable,
virginal and sexless, forever ahead and behind.
We conceive a lover as we conceive a child
not knowing the result.

Form really is distinct from what it contains.
That one person can witness another
with eye and ear and hand
suffers each to liberate each
from the self-ignorance
of wrongly
construed inwardness.
We are rescued into the relief of the round.

That's how wind grasps in advance
the midsummer maple-crowns sucking
their green suspirations from them,
how seawater knowingly mouths the oscillant
ovals of heavenly purples and blues,
how Galatea predicts and accommodates
the coursing of Pygmalion's fingers
though (through her mercy) he may attribute
the perfect justice of the sensation
to the replete kneading and skimming of his love,
like a thirsty swallow that sips from a lake on the wing.

4.

Galatea had been quarried of the living stone.
Vitality preceded Pygmalion, only rock
dropped away. He thought his hands
wrought a change, but he altered
nothing: so from their blind
nests the migrants
absorb all the starry
sky above them.
The law of navigation impends
beyond the bristly rim of their wild cradle,
but they never patterned the night.

Pygmalion's embrace. The tepescence of Galatea.
Both responded, more malleably still, to a third thing
that explained how the advent of such strength
is softness.

To explain how the advent of such strength
is softness, what must be asked is what
is it to have the permission of Venus?

5.

The uncreated hands of Pygmalion were made
by the force that fleshed Galatea's breasts,
her armpits, her thighs and her throat's
tense beauties and her face
lifted and reddened and the smile
swung away beyond it, so high
and the rims of her teeth gleamed
in disclosure—Galatea revealed
his fingers and his eyes
and the crush and glide of their encompassing
made of her just then
the immersion that dissolved
the clumsy chisel's metal into flesh.

The author wishes to acknowledge *The Antigonish Review, Bei Mei Feng, Canadian Literature, The Dalhousie Review, The Fiddlehead, Landmarks, The Malahat Review, The Nashwaak Review* and *Vallum* for publishing some of these poems. Thanks also to Monique Dull, Iain Higgins, Ross Leckie and Luke Carson.

ALSO BY ERIC MILLER

POETRY

Song of the Vulgar Starling
In the Scaffolding

ESSAYS

The Reservoir

TRANSLATIONS

Nemesis Divina
(from the Swedish of Linnaeus)

Dialogues on the Beauty of Nature
(from the German of Johann Georg Sulzer)

We Are Like Fire
(from the German of Wilhelm Waiblinger and Herman Hesse)

Rapture of the Depths
(from the German of Bettina Klix)